A BOWL OF WARM AIR

By the same author:

The Country at My Shoulder (1993)

A BOWL OF WARM AIR

Moniza Alvi

Oxford   New York
OXFORD UNIVERSITY PRESS
1996

Oxford University Press, Walton Street, Oxford OX2 6DP

Oxford New York
Athens Auckland Bangkok Bombay
Calcutta Cape Town Dar es Salaam Delhi
Florence Hong Kong Istanbul Karachi
Kuala Lumpur Madras Madrid Melbourne
Mexico City Nairobi Paris Singapore
Taipei Tokyo Toronto
and associated companies in
Berlin Ibadan

Oxford is a trade mark of Oxford University Press

First published in Oxford Poets
as an Oxford University Press paperback 1996

British Library Cataloguing in Publication Data
Data available

Library of Congress Cataloging in Publication Data
Alvi, Moniza.
A bowl of warm air / Moniza Alvi.
p. cm.
1. Pakistan—Poetry. I. Title.
PR9540.9.A55B69 1996   821'.914—dc20   95-36144
ISBN 0-19-282520-8

1 3 5 7 9 10 8 6 4 2

Typeset by Rowland Phototypesetting Limited
Printed in Hong Kong

For Bob

ACKNOWLEDGEMENTS

Acknowledgements are due to the editors of the following publications in which some of these poems first appeared: *As Girls Could Boast* (The Oscars Press), *Klaonica—Poems for Bosnia* (Bloodaxe), *The Observer*, *New Writing 5* (Vintage), *London Magazine*, *Poetry London Newsletter*, *Poetry Review*, *The Rialto*, *Scratch* and *Wasafiri*.

'Story of a City' was commissioned by The London Arts Board.

I would especially like to thank Christina Dunhill for her assistance with this collection.

CONTENTS

I

And If   3
The Double City   4
Hindi Urdu Bol Chaal   6
Fighter Planes   8
The Wedding   9
The Airborne House   11
My Father's Father's Father   12
The Courtyard   13
An Unknown Girl   14
My Aunts Don't Want to Move   16
Shoes and Socks   17
The Colours of the World   18
Grand Hotel   20
Lahore Canal   21
Rolling   22
Where Have You Been?   24
Delhi Christmas   25
Rainy Season   26
O Maharani   27
The Laughing Moon   30

II

Exile   33
Under the Brick   34
Houdini   35
The Illusionist   36
Women of this World   37
Burial   38
A Bowl of Warm Air   39
Moving In   40
Our House   41
Afterlife   42
My Prehistoric Name   43
All There Is   44
Story of a City   45
Tuning In   46

I

AND IF

If you could choose a country
to belong to—
perhaps you had one
snatched away,
once offered to you
like a legend
in a basket covered with a cloth—

and if the sun were a simple flare,
the streets beating out
the streets, and your breath
lost on the road
with the Yadavs, herding cattle,
then you could rest, absorb
it all in the cool of the hills,

but still you might peel back one face
to retrieve another
and another, down to the face that is
unbearable, so clear
so complex, hinting at nations,
castes and sub-castes
and you would touch it once—

and if this Eastern track were
a gusty English lane
where rain makes mirrors
in the holes,
a rat lies lifeless, sodden
as an old floorcloth,
you'd be untouchable—as one

defined by someone else—
one who cleans the toilets,
burns the dead.

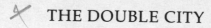 THE DOUBLE CITY

I live in one city,
but then it becomes another.
The point where they mesh—
I call it mine.

Dacoits creep from caves
in the banks of the Indus.

One of them is displaced.
From Trafalgar Square
he dominates London, his face
masked by scarves and sunglasses.
He draws towards him all the conflict
of the metropolis—his speech
a barrage of grenades, rocket-launchers.

He marks time with his digital watch.
The pigeons get under his feet.

In the double city the beggar's cry
travels from one region to the next.

Under sapphire skies
or muscular clouds
there are fluid streets
and solid streets.
On some it is safe to walk.

The women of Southall
champion the release
of the battered Kiranjit
who killed her husband.
Lord Taylor, free her now!
Their saris billow in a storm of chants.

4

Schoolchildren of many nationalities
enact the Ramayana.
The princely Rama
fights with demons
while the monkey god
searches for Princess Sita.

I make discoveries and lose them
little by little.
My journey in the double city
starts beneath my feet.
You are here, says the arrow.

HINDI URDU BOL CHAAL

(*bol chaal*: dialogue)

These are languages I try to touch
as if my tongue is a fingertip gently
matching its whorls to echoings of sound.

Separating Urdu from Hindi—it's like
sifting grains of wild rice
or separating India from Pakistan.

The sign of nasal intonation
floats like a heat haze
above new words.

Words like hands banging on the table.

*

I introduce myself to two languages,
but there are so many—of costume,
of conduct and courtesy.

I listen hard as if to sense minute
changes of dialect from village to village
from West Punjab to West Bengal.

These languages could have been mine—
the whisper of silks on silks
and the slapping and patting of chapattis on the tava.

*

I imagine the meetings and greetings
in Urdu borrowed from Sanskrit,
Arabic and Persian.

I shall be borrowed from England.
Pakistan, assalaam alaikum—
Peace be with you—Helloji.

It is not you I am meeting.
It is a sound system travelling through
countries, ascending and descending

in ragas, drumbeats, clapping.

*

In Lahore there grows a language tree
its roots branching to an earlier time
its fruit ripe, ready to fall.

I hear the rustling of mango groves
my living and dead relatives
quarrelling together and I search

for a nugget of sound, the kernel
of language. I am enlarged
by what I cannot hear—

the village conferences, the crackling
of bonfires and the rap of gunfire.

*

My senses stir with words
that must be reinvented.
At the market I'll ask *How much?*

and wait for just one new word
to settle like a stone
at the bottom of a well.

FIGHTER PLANES

I saw the bright
green parrots
make their nests
in fighter planes,
thought I could fly
and peck at little
bits of the world,
beat my wings
where I was born

try looping lines
between the hemispheres.

THE WEDDING

I expected a quiet wedding
high above a lost city
a marriage to balance on my head

like a forest of sticks, a pot of water.
The ceremony tasted of nothing
had little colour—guests arrived

stealthy as sandalwood smugglers.
When they opened their suitcases
England spilled out.

They scratched at my veil
like beggars on a car window.
I insisted my dowry was simple—

a smile, a shadow, a whisper,
my house an incredible structure
of stiffened rags and bamboo.

We travelled along roads with English
names, my bridegroom and I.
Our eyes changed colour

like traffic-lights, so they said.
The time was not ripe
for us to view each other.

We stared straight ahead as if
we could see through mountains
breathe life into new cities.

I wanted to marry a country
take up a river for a veil
sing in the Jinnah Gardens

hold up my dream, tricky
as a snake-charmer's snake.
Our thoughts half-submerged

like buffaloes under dark water
we turned and faced each other
with turbulence

and imprints like maps on our hands.

THE AIRBORNE HOUSE

Ceiling fans whirl like helicopters
as if this house is about to take off—

And it does!
Servants, prepared for smiling

are whisked upwards, clasping jugs
of salted lemonade—and this house

this bulwark against the sunlight glare
floats clean away, leaving in its wake

vying carhorns, chants of street vendors,
the gradations of Delhi poor.

Hospitable ladies busy themselves
while rocking in the upper atmosphere.

They tell the servants what to do,
debate whether it is better

to have them sleeping near you or not.
And the girls tackle homework—

in English (Hindi's not allowed at school).
Everyone agrees it's been too hot

to penetrate the shops at Connaught Circus.
Tiger, the labrador bought from Harrods

trouble with his back legs,
stumbles through the airborne cool

and sinks down on the marble floor.

MY FATHER'S FATHER'S FATHER

In this city I have aged thousands of years.
I am older than the oldest tree in the world.

There are homes here for ancient holy cows
but none for old people, nowhere for me to go.

It is good that like the cows I am prepared
to wander the lanes and alleyways.

I was here before my father's father's father—
I think I can identify him, rising upwards

like K2 on an early relief map of India.
He is so old his skin is flaking like leaves,

his hair is soft as dust. I take his arm,
tell him who I am, then we are old together.

We vow to bathe ourselves everyday although
we are so old, because like the city

we are hanging by a tough thread
and dead-looking trees

have brilliant purple flowers.

THE COURTYARD

Stepping across to a whitewashed room, you look up
and unexpectedly the ceiling is the sky, with a single
star, its rays like the spokes of a wall clock.
At once you notice there is plenty of meat for guests
at the long table, despite the butchers' strike.

Then drifting past the melon, the tutti-frutti ice-cream
is it a child who helps herself to bottled water?
At the same time she grows and ages.
She speaks more than one language—each fades
like writing in air and gives way to another.

She gestures to a side door—to the wedding bedroom
silvered with tinsel and glass baubles,
bunches of dried flowers in wallpaper formation.
The bride smiles shyly amidst Western-style furniture.
And the child darts off and loses herself

in the dark corners of the courtyard,
the hills of washing waiting for the dhobi.

AN UNKNOWN GIRL

In the evening bazaar
studded with neon
an unknown girl
is hennaing my hand.
She squeezes a wet brown line
from a nozzle.
She is icing my hand,
which she steadies with hers
on her satin-peach knee.
In the evening bazaar
for a few rupees
an unknown girl
is hennaing my hand.
As a little air catches
my shadow-stitched kameez
a peacock spreads its lines
across my palm.
Colours leave the street
float up in balloons.
Dummies in shop-fronts
tilt and stare
with their Western perms.
Banners for Miss India 1993,
for curtain cloth
and sofa cloth
canopy me.
I have new brown veins.
In the evening bazaar
very deftly
an unknown girl
is hennaing my hand.
I am clinging
to these firm peacock lines
like people who cling
to the sides of a train.
Now the furious streets
are hushed.

I'll scrape off
the dry brown lines
before I sleep,
reveal soft as a snail trail
the amber bird beneath.
It will fade in a week.
When India appears and reappears
I'll lean across a country
with my hands outstretched
longing for the unknown girl
in the neon bazaar.

MY AUNTS DON'T WANT TO MOVE

They hug their house around them
half-underground in a deafening city,
hurry across the yellow courtyard
with its waxy plants and coverless bed
where no one sleeps, sweats and turns
by doors to secret, sombre rooms.

Their house contracts and holds them.
Its simple brocade sitting-room
where uncle, father, brother preside—
they face each other on the mantelshelf.
The Alpine picture, the dividing curtain
women draw when unknown men appear.

They revolve their house before them.
It turns itself inside out.
The ancient wiring, knee-high stoves,
continuous stream of delicacies,
the bruising bangles waiting in the drawer—
just visible on the brink of the world.

SHOES AND SOCKS

In the vast forecourt of the Badshahi Mosque
my cousin pulls off his trainers.
I've never seen so many holes in socks!

The exhibits here are shoes and socks
temporarily abandoned by their owners,
a little hope tied in the laces—

Ali Baba sandals, business shoes
all precious to the shoe-keeper.
Azam's socks have gaping holes,

one for each of his teenage years?
And through them slip his studies,
political career, his rebellion,

his dutiful laying of the table.
Religion rumbles through the holes,
the insistent cry of the muezzin,

fears of what will happen to him if
he sleeps with a girl before marriage
and is discovered . . .

Those who desire to fulfil their desires,
or wish to free themselves of desire,
leave their footwear paraded on the steps,

each shoe a small vessel for prayer.
Trainers for the new world, the old world.
In sight of the towering gateway—

the earthbound shoes and socks.

THE COLOURS OF THE WORLD

It is time, almost time
    for her to leave her house.

It is not normally done
    for a woman to go out alone
except to the bazaar
    to buy rat traps or garlands.
She glows within her body
    like the model of the Taj
inside the Red Fort.
    She reads her sacred script
which flows like water,
    recalls her husband's words—
From my first wife
    there was no issue.
She yearns to place
    a block on cloth, strike it
with a mallet—one blow
    for each of her children.

She ponders the miniatures
    glimpsed in the museum.
The heroine watching
    violet, raging clouds.
Moghul ladies playing polo.
    While outside the rain falls—
the white, the sapphire,
    the blood-red drops
spreading into lakes.

She will leave her house.

She'll go to the bank
    and see for herself
how air-conditioning
    turns it into a palace.

She dreams the women
        are singing, bursting
in the red-light area, Hiramundi,
        while she rubs her face
against a map of the world.

She's a woman with modest dress,
        but when she goes out
the men will stare—
        she'll be conspicuous
like a Western woman.

The fullness of her clothes
        will swirl around her—
when the colours of the world
        rush out to meet her.

GRAND HOTEL

This is how life began—
with a Grand Hotel propelled
into the middle of India,

breathing fire and ice,
sucking in the world
and hurling it away.

All the living organisms roll
on the bed with stomach pains.
The bathroom almost gleams.

The carpet smells
of something old and fried,
though incense burns.

Mock princes hover at tables,
poorly paid, return
to shacks and open drains,

serve the invaders, oddly white
and semi-clad, armed with
sticks and cameras and maps.

LAHORE CANAL

As I glimpse the agile boys
plunging into the Lahore Canal
escaping the torment of the sun,
I imagine myself a girl here
one slow, stifling afternoon
inside with the shutters closed—
rather bored, a little mystified
picking up another English novel
which begins *It was a glorious day,
the hottest for weeks . . .*

ROLLING

In my dreams I roll
like the holy man
who rolls two thousand miles
down the middle of the highway
who rolls for eight months
to a Himalayan Shrine.
In my dreams I roll—
A battered van follows me
girls dance beside me
trucks overturn.
I'll roll like a map
like a bale of cloth.
No one will turn their head
no one will say
You can't roll here.
I'll spin through India's
hundred millions
pass through my father's house
before he fled to Pakistan
roll through my family name.
I'll roll right into the girl
I might have been
growing up here.
I'll roll in the day and night.
I'll hold a scarf
taut between my hands
to steer through this world
of sharp stones, fine dust
bullocks like rocks
at the roadside.
I roll beneath advertisements
for Cadbury's Chocolate,
the road warnings
Life is Short,
Don't make it any Shorter.
And someone is calling out
How much is a shoe
in England these days?

My dreams, my bandaged elbows!
I'm rotating beneath the neem trees
by ancient monuments.
I'm wriggling through stars in fretwork.
And as I roll the city rolls.
Rolls through a vision of myself
in the undifferentiated crowd.
The shacks, the rag-roof shelters roll
the donkeys with their impossible loads.
And in my ear the small scrape
of the roadside barber's razor.
I roll past women
cutting cane in the mud
women combing long dyed hair.
I gather all the smells and sounds
like a shawl around me.
I'm revolving on my axis
churning like butter or ghee
whirled along by chanting

until I arrive—

Somewhere I think I might have been
but it's not a Himalayan shrine
and no goddess expects me.
Only the young and the old are carried
so I'll walk the last yards
and then I'll stand and wait
with everyone else.
I'll touch my bandaged elbows
very lightly, my headache fading
and remember only
how I rolled ten miles a day.

WHERE HAVE YOU BEEN?

My camera had been filled with the details
of moghul monuments, but now it put its nose
in the rubbish where the holy cow
and the beggar who walks on all fours
cast their shadows—it nuzzled plastic bags,
smelt putrefying fruit—the lens wobbled,
elongating like an elephant's trunk.
All the odours are in the camera's stomach
continually churning and swilling,
with the woman who sifts through litter
searching as if it could take forever—
for a baby, for gold, for edible fruit.

Oh where have you been, my camera, my son?
Oh where have you been my one-eyed young man?

DELHI CHRISTMAS

In hotel lobbies skinny Christmas trees
rest on beds of egg-white satin

hold blunt finger-strips of cotton wool.
Santa gestures like a tour leader

next to log cabin, jewelled caravan.
Piano and cello send incessant *Jingle Bells*

into the costly international atmosphere.
And *The Times of India* hosts recipes

for 'ginger hut' and marzipan.
Inhabitants of silent corridors—the workers

murmur Merry Christmas, nod and smile.
Fierce air-conditioning creates a winter chill.

Sunbathers, indolent, line the swimming pool,
while England floats contained, so far away

like a glass-domed scene with shaken snow.
Cliff-like in the cool night air

Eastern hotels tap lightly into Christmas.
English couples talk of cats in Abingdon.

RAINY SEASON

I scale the wall
walk the tightrope high above
the house where I was born.
The neighbourhood dips beneath me
and the wind blows.

Daytime the sky is white and cool
as a bowl of firni.
Night time it flows like a woman's hair.
I conjure up the rainy season, command each drop
set this house like an ark on the ocean.

O MAHARANI

There was a place for me in the miniature.
Someone had taken the trouble to sketch in

my features with fine strokes from a brush
of chipmunk's tail, and my clothes surged

with brushstrokes from camel's eyebrow.
Sometimes the scene reminded me of England

with English paperweights set in mirrorwork.
Mostly I heard the artificial rainy season—

fountains in the Girlfriends' Garden.
I slipped on wetness at the edge of a pool

to the amusement of Ahmedabad schoolboys.
Then India opened its immense eyes

and I stepped out of the frame.

*

It was difficult to know how to cope
away from the painting.

Although I grew taller and plumper
I was soon lost in the raging crowds.

I raced on and on to escape and
was confronted by walls of fortresses

corridors and inner courtyards.
At last I found a Chamber of Audience

and a maharani who'd designed
a tale of India and England

for a patterned carpet
which changed landscapes

as you walked on it,
and was at first India

which melted into England
and then became

England mixed with India.
A knotted carpet

that could never catch fire.
There is such an emotional scene

enthused this queen
When a newly woven carpet leaves home.

And she passed on stories to me
as she'd passed on costumes

to her maidservants
patchwork kameez with hidden pockets.

I felt the weight of her stories.
Take something back to England

she insisted.
There was a maharaja who took with him

Ganges' water for drinking.
Perhaps you'd like a set of tiger claws?

Or stay here, so far from home.
Be like the rickshaw driver without lights

in the dark and smoke and grit.
You'd get used to it.

Then I thought of my beginnings
and sang

O Maharani
I'd rather be like the miniaturist who works alone
Painting on rice paper, silk and camel bone
Polishing an image with a stone.

THE LAUGHING MOON

I had two pillows and one was England,
two cheeks and one was England.

Pakistan held me and dropped me in the night.
I slid through
           yesterday and tomorrow—

An unknown country crept between
my toes, threw an ocean behind my eye.
I couldn't tell whether the sky was red
or green, cotton or silk and if it would tear.

I could see myself spinning like an important
message through a hole to the other side
           of the world.

I'd held out my arms to kingfishers and tigers,
I'd sipped each moment like a language,
touched something I knew better
than my own parcel-weight.

Shakily England picked me up
           with her grey fingers.
England had a cure for everything
stuck between the bricks of houses.

The continents were very old,
but I was new and breathing in
           midnight,

the laughing moon in its place.

II

EXILE

The old land swinging in her stomach
she must get to know this language
better—key words, sound patterns
wordgroups of fire and blood.

Try your classmates with
the English version of your name.
Maria. Try it.
Good afternoon. How are you?

I am fine. Your country—
you see it in a drop of water.
The last lesson they taught you there
was how to use a gun.

And now in stops and starts
you grow a second city in your head.
It is Christmas in this school.
Sarajevo is falling through

a forest of lit-up trees,
cards and decorations.
Mountains split with gunfire
swallow clouds, birds, sky.

UNDER THE BRICK

Concealed beneath a wasteland brick
a creased black-and-white photograph
of coupling—and we'd retrieve it
on those everlasting walks from school.
We'd turn it this way, that way, unsure
exactly how a couple fitted together,
put it back under the brick, but each day
find it again below the steel grey sky,
the London Country buses passing.
We'd pause, speechless, tilt our heads,
while their missing heads lived in
another world, outside the photograph.

At night I'd dream
and under the gritty newtown stars
the brick would hold down our secret,
would press on the headless bodies,
the limbs and their arrested activity,
the flesh more cracked and creased.

The lone couple, untouched by moonlight—
tiny creatures under a brick
in the middle of the wasteland.

HOUDINI

It is not clear how he entered me
or why he always has to escape.
Maybe he's just proving to the crowds
he can still do it—He whispers
half-words which bloom in the dark
Ma ha ma ha.

Sometimes he feeds me cough medicine.
Or bathes his genitals in salt water.
Then heaves his body upwards
as if pressing against a lid.
At least he prefers me
to his underwater box, to the manacles
which clank on his moon-white skin.
I wonder what it is exactly
he sees within me?
He touches my insides as though
he'd sighted the first landplants—
I'm catching cloud between my fingers.

Tonight the wind whips through my stomach
over knots of trees and sharp rocks.
When he rushes out of me the crowd gasps—
and I implode from sheer emptiness.

THE ILLUSIONIST

He saws her in half—widthways, lengthways
and proclaims she's his finest illusion

when part of her is somewhere else
across the other side of the room.

He prowls up and down the echoey stage-set
and produces a baby out of shimmering air.

Then he flies off like Peter Pan, and returns
with all her lost boyfriends, like the first

who loved to drive cars backwards
and the fourth, with pre-Raphaelite hair.

But next he abandons the whole adventure
to twirl a floating head in a tank.

It's bleak in his absence, her absence—
she feels that he's hijacked her soul.

Until he cycles back on a wheel like the sun
and surveys her with undisguised interest.

He kisses her, stopping just long enough to
explain how once he made an aeroplane disappear.

WOMEN OF THIS WORLD

Some women of this world
have my fingerprints running along
just below the surface of their skin.

Some women to whom I lent my clothes
are wearing them beneath the skin—
linen, rayon, watered silks.

Threading in and out of their skin
like a needle and bright cotton
go my fantasies, my finest hopes.

I interview myself severely,
handcuff my dreams to a mountain
which seems to fit their description.

I am seeking some women of this world.
I have come for my fingerprints—
I have come to take them away.

BURIAL

He'll bury her in the garden bit by bit
an eyebrow under an orange bush
her breasts below the rockery
and lay her smile across the gravel path
go up and down with the watering-can—

So every part of her will flourish
and her scent will overtake him
until he tells the world to stop—
and something of what she is
will fall into his arms.

A BOWL OF WARM AIR

Someone is falling towards you
as an apple falls from a branch,
moving slowly, imperceptibly as if
into a new political epoch,
or excitedly like a dog towards a bone.
He is holding in both hands
everything he knows he has—
a bowl of warm air.

He has sighted you from afar
as if you were a dramatic crooked tree
on the horizon and he has seen you close up
like the underside of a mushroom.
But he cannot open you like a newspaper
or put you down like a newspaper.

And you are satisfied that he is veering towards you
and that he is adjusting his speed
and that the sun and the wind and rain are in front of him
and the sun and the wind and rain are behind him.

MOVING IN

I think within me there's a space
where organs, muscles, blood
have just moved out
and you've moved in
with your exhilarating bird
your honest stone
a chunk of land
a slice of cliff—
I know it could be easy
to turn inside out
then cautiously propel me
through the waiting world
where everyone will see
how changed I am—
and gazing at the bird
assorted rock and stone
not know exactly
what to say or do.

OUR HOUSE

Our house will have a parrot in the sink,
a horse cavorting in the living-room.
A thousand animal presences will canter
through the unaccustomed quiet.
In this house we'll borrow one another's
stomachs, one another's sighs, and listen
to the milk which starts to separate.

When the shadows of my domain overlap
the shadows of yours, nothing will stand still,
even the pictures will skate across the walls,
their phantoms tilt and speak.
of ripened afternoons, unveiling, dying.
Our agile house with smeared windows
where fireworks explode off the computer screen—

Change is a tremor in our wrists, our groans.
The carpet rolls unswervingly across the floor,
the ceilings whiten like cool skies.
We've alcoves of sad furniture, a hall of jokes,
telegrams with no messages, and on the pillows
those strange frogs, smaller than their tadpoles.
We are too slight for this brave place—

It is eating us, then we're ingesting it.
Our tour of its rooms will never end—
the first house ever built, our vaulted space,
The House That Jack Built, House of Usher.
We creep up to the doors, ensure they are doors
then light as insects
frolic in the dustbeams on the stairs.

AFTERLIFE

Like oranges we roll right off the table.
I am lost as a goldfish stuck in sky.
No news of you, but I cry out
and you appear, carrying a photograph

of life-tormented trees—how glad we are
to see our old stiff selves released
sucked down, and melting at the seams.
We'll make the mistakes we wished we'd made.

They say the soul might have some choice—
I could for instance be a taste or smell,
something sharp curled on the tongue.
You and I as leopard breath or song.

MY PREHISTORIC NAME

I'm pulling myself out of one of my lives
as if I were an old tooth.

I'm calling up who I was yesterday
and what I was a hundred years ago.

I'll hurl myself down like a wildcard—
sitting here I've almost ceased to breathe.

Now the horse is in the igloo
and the rabbit's in the stable.

When the horse bolts I'll go with him
clinging to the tassels of his mane,

trailing remnants of a street, a dialect,
my childhood schemes, and I'll whisper

and repeat my prehistoric name.

ALL THERE IS

The stars are spiderlike
drawn by adults
who long to draw
like children—
and these are the child's
unanchored rooftops, hills.
The moon ticks like a clock.

The woman hugging herself
on her firm bed
dreams of a gay man
she knows slightly,
boyish, thin and dark
singing the mellowest song
she ever heard.

Yesterday she ran out of bread,
ran out of almost everything.
And now this dream
with all there is to see
and all there is to smell
undoing itself
on the fluid side of time.

STORY OF A CITY

I could tell you the story of a city—
how I seduced it in the afternoon.
The silenced birds were tangled in its hair.

I tried to stroke its million arms, its domes,
swept off some dust and sweetened it with rain,
unwound the suffocating scarves of dirt,

pounded it like a drum, like carnival time,
watched it stretch until it burst
with rhythm, paint and revelry and song.

Calming the city, subduing it in my house,
I thought I'd store it high up on a shelf,
or slip it in my pocket like a pen.

I begged on its behalf—a coin, a stroke of luck—
then left it in the dark recesses of a shop
steadily receding to another continent,

retrieved its deserts, chasms, embryos,
its open squares and theatre steps,
observed its networks running in my hands.

I started to examine how it seemed to be
just stuffed and stuffed inside itself.
Though once I cracked it open like an egg—

heard the river roaring free, the named
and nameless threats, the interlocking worlds.
At night I lie with this uncharted city.

It turns to me and murmurs in its sleep
I need you. Make of me what you can—
my suburbs of ideas, my flames, my empty spaces.

TUNING IN

Now for the morning story,
or in the afternoon that tale
of adventurous, practical children.
Ship ahoy! Time for a new mooring.

With no special interest in boats
I tune in to the vivid location.
Something disappears on the airwaves.
Tendrils of spring are twining

across the electromagnetic field.
Comedy bubbles up from the archives.
Some of us listen, heads bent
as if in search of a lost item—

until a voice whirls and grips us.
We eat it up like an apple.
We are the indoor people, all ears—
disturbance is detected from afar.

Leaves crackling at the window.
The vibration of tremendous journeys.

OXFORD POETS

Fleur Adcock
Moniza Alvi
Kamau Brathwaite
Joseph Brodsky
Basil Bunting
Daniela Crăsnaru
Michael Donaghy
Keith Douglas
D. J. Enright
Roy Fisher
Ida Affleck Graves
Ivor Gurney
David Harsent
Gwen Harwood
Anthony Hecht
Zbigniew Herbert
Thomas Kinsella
Brad Leithauser
Derek Mahon
Jamie McKendrick

Sean O'Brien
Alice Oswald
Peter Porter
Craig Raine
Zsuzsa Rakovszky
Henry Reed
Christopher Reid
Stephen Romer
Carole Satyamurti
Peter Scupham
Jo Shapcott
Penelope Shuttle
Anne Stevenson
George Szirtes
Grete Tartler
Edward Thomas
Charles Tomlinson
Marina Tsvetaeva
Chris Wallace-Crabbe
Hugo Williams